For Tara Aspen and Noël Sedona, my sunshine.
—D. C.

To my parents, Rob and Tina Moeckel,
for their gift of music.
—A. C.

Text copyright © 2022 Donna Cangelosi. Illustrations copyright © 2022 Amanda Calatzis. First published in 2022 by Page Street Kids,
an imprint of Page Street Publishing Co., 27 Congress Street, Suite 1511, Salem, MA 01970, www.pagestreetpublishing.com.
All rights reserved. No part of this book may be reproduced or used, in any form or by any means, electronic or mechanical, without
prior permission in writing from the publisher. Distributed by Macmillan, sales in Canada by The Canadian Manda Group.
ISBN-13: 978-1-64567-470-2. ISBN-10: 1-64567-470-3. CIP data for this book is available from the Library of Congress. This book was
typeset in Ashbury Light. The illustrations were done in watercolor, gouache, acrylics, colored pencil, graphite, and digital media.
Cover and book design by Julia Tyler for Page Street Kids. Printed and bound in Shenzhen, Guangdong, China.
22 23 24 25 26 CCO 5 4 3 2

Page Street Publishing uses only materials from suppliers who are committed to responsible and sustainable forest management.
Page Street Publishing protects our planet by donating to nonprofits like The Trustees, which focuses on local land conservation.

Mister Rogers'
Gift of Music

Donna Cangelosi

illustrated by Amanda Calatzis

PAGE
STREET
KIDS

Fred Rogers looked directly into the television camera.
He smiled and sang as if every child in America was in the
room with him. . . .

Miles away, north and south, east and west of his Pittsburgh studio, thousands of children throughout the United States tuned in to *Mister Rogers' Neighborhood*. Each child felt like Mister Rogers was singing just to them.

They sang along like a neighborhood choir—together even though they were miles apart.

A beautiful day, for a neighbor.

Would you be mine?

Could you be mine?

Fred hoped music would help children as much as it helped him when he was a young boy—spending long days alone in his room, watching his neighbors play in the warm sun while he was stuck inside wheezing with asthma.

Then one day the enchanting sound of Grandfather McFeely's violin spiraled up the stairs to young Fred's room. The melody lifted his spirits above the fog of sickness. Fred's loneliness drifted away.

Music was sunshine.

By the time Fred was five, he found his own way to make sunshine. His fingers danced across the keys of a piano and swirls of sounds filled his days. Before long, Fred could hear a tune on the radio and play it, without a single flaw.

But sometimes, loud chuckles and name-calling from other kids drowned the jingles. A storm of dark feelings rumbled inside Fred's heart, trying to find a way out.

Young Fred tapped the keys and learned to play the sounds of his feelings. Soft sinking sobs, loud rippling roars, and trickles of teardrops flowed through his fingertips. Making music pushed Fred's gloomy feelings out and let fresh air in. Through the years, Fred's piano became a friend he could always turn to.

Fred loved singing and playing his piano alone, but he didn't want to keep his melodies all to himself. He wanted to share them with children—to brighten their lives, too. So, with a tune in his head, a trunkful of sweaters and puppets, and a toy trolley, he created *Mister Rogers' Neighborhood.*

Through the power of television, he shared hundreds of songs he wrote as gifts for kids.

What do you do with

Sometimes the children Fred sang to inspired him to write new songs, too. One day, Fred received a letter from a child. "What do you do with the mad that you feel when you feel so mad you could bite?"

Fred knew angry, sad, and scared emotions are part of growing up. He didn't want children to ignore or hold them in. Whenever he felt angry or upset, Fred sat at the piano and made it boom! So he raced to his piano and wrote a song.

Playing the piano didn't only help Fred express his feelings. Creating springy jingles and soft serenades sparked his creativity and sense of wonder. It felt like floating on a cloud.

To open up that magical world for kids, Fred introduced a rainbow of fascinating instruments. And he invited spectacular musicians to perform.

Famous trumpeter Wynton Marsalis spun notes into a weeping melody and made playful pitches pop.

Cellist Yo-Yo Ma created tones that flowed like a graceful swan and raging rhythms that roared like a lion.

And when the neighborhood guitarist, Mr. Negri, joined him, Fred sang along. Their harmony felt as comforting as a warm hug.

Tree, tree, tree

Tree, tree, tree

We love you

But Fred's greatest gifts to children were the lyrics of his songs. Knowing the feeling of being an outsider, Fred made everyone feel special. Sick kids, lonely kids, kids who didn't fit in.

Everyone.

You are my friend You are special

You are my friend

You are my friend

You're special to me

Everywhere Fred went, kids young and old sang to him.
In crowded subway cars, while speaking at graduations,
and when receiving a star on Hollywood Boulevard.
They sang and sang like a neighborhood choir—together,
even though they had grown up miles and years apart.

It's a beautiful day in this neighborhood.

Music *was* sunshine! And Fred spread enough not only for an entire neighborhood, but for an entire country for generations.

A beautiful day for a neighbor. Would you be mine? Could you be mine?

Thirty-three years after starting *Mister Rogers' Neighborhood*, Fred entered his studio for the last time. He looked directly into the camera and smiled. And because Fred liked to say things with music, he gave his television neighbors a final gift.

It's such a good feeling

Author's Note

What makes Mister Rogers' songs so timeless? Perhaps the memory of his grandfather's violin? The bouncy beats he grew up hearing on the radio? Or is it something bigger, something from deep inside his heart?

Fred McFeely Rogers was born in 1928. During his long days stuck inside with asthma, Fred's mother often played the piano to cheer him up. Soon, Fred also learned to play and noticed that music was a great way to express his emotions. He once said, "[Music] was always my way of saying who I was and how I felt. I was always able to cry or laugh or say I was angry through the tips of my fingers on the piano."

When Fred was about ten, his grandmother Nancy McFeely bought him his first piano. Fred poured his feelings into that piano his entire life, including during his music composition studies in college.

Mister Rogers' Neighborhood first aired in 1968. Throughout the 895 episodes filmed, Fred showed kids unwavering love and understanding that no other creator of children's music has matched. His songs about growing up, feelings, and respecting one another have pulled people together, like an invisible thread of love and kindness—which never goes out of style.

In 2012, nine years after Fred Rogers died, Fred Rogers Productions introduced the animated series *Daniel Tiger's Neighborhood*, featuring the son of Fred's puppet Daniel Striped Tiger. Like Fred, Daniel Tiger starts each episode singing, "It's a beautiful day in the neighborhood…" And a new generation of children sings along.

Bibliography

Cangelosi, Donna. Telephone interview and email communications with Emily Uhrin, Archive Director, Fred Rogers Center. December 12, 2017; February 16, 2018; June 22, 2021.

Herman, Karen. "Archive of American Television Interview with Fred Rogers." July 22, 1999. https://interviews.televisionacademy.com/interviews/fred-rogers?clip=48374#interview-clips.

Junod, Tom. "Can You Say . . . Hero?" *Esquire*. November 1998, 132–38.

Kimmel, Margaret M., and Mark Collins. *The Wonder of It All: Fred Rogers and the Story of an Icon*. Latrobe, PA: Fred Rogers Center, 2008.

King, Maxwell. *The Good Neighbor: The Life and Work of Fred Rogers*. New York: Abrams, 2018.

Laskas, J. M. "The Mister Rogers No One Saw." *New York Times*. November 19, 2019. https://www.nytimes.com/2019/11/19/magazine/mr-rogers.html.

Pittsburgh Music History. "The Music of Fred Rogers." January 9, 2019. https://sites.google.com/site/pittsburghmusichistory/pittsburgh-music-story/pop/fred-rogers.

Rogers, Fred. *Dear Mister Rogers: Does It Ever Rain in Your Neighborhood? Letters to Mister Rogers*. New York: Penguin, 1996.

Rogers, Fred. "It's Such a Good Feeling." The Neighborhood Archive. Accessed December 1, 2019. http://www.neighborhoodarchive.com/music/songs/its_such_a_good_feeling.html.

Rogers, Fred. "Tree Tree Tree." The Neighborhood Archive. Accessed December 1, 2019. http://www.neighborhoodarchive.com/music/songs/tree_tree_tree.html.

Rogers, Fred. "What Do You Do With the Mad That You Feel?" The Neighborhood Archive. Accessed December 1, 2019. http://www.neighborhoodarchive.com/music/songs/what_do_you_do.html.

Rogers, Fred. "Won't You Be My Neighbor?" The Neighborhood Archive. Accessed December 1, 2019. http://www.neighborhoodarchive.com/music/songs/wont_you_be_my_neighbor.html.

Rogers, Fred. "You Are My Friend." The Neighborhood Archive. Accessed December 1, 2019. http://www.neighborhoodarchive.com/music/songs/tree_tree_tree.html.